CIRCUS AMERICANA
and
OTHER POEMS

Also by Michael Scofield from Sunstone Press

Acting Badly
Making Crazy
Smut Busters
Whirling Backward Into the World

Sunstone books may be purchased for educational, business, or sales promotional use.
For information please write: Special Markets Department, Sunstone Press,
P.O. Box 2321, Santa Fe, New Mexico 87504-2321.

Book and cover design › Vicki Ahl
Body typeface › Californian FB
Printed on acid-free paper
∞
eBook 978-1-61139-326-2

Library of Congress Cataloging-in-Publication Data
Scofield, Michael.
[Poems. Selections]
Circus americana : and other poems / by Michael Scofield.
    pages ; cm
ISBN 978-1-63293-028-6 (softcover : acid-free paper)
I. Title.
PS3619.C63A6 2014
811'.6--dc23

                              2014033653

WWW.SUNSTONEPRESS.COM
SUNSTONE PRESS / POST OFFICE BOX 2321 / SANTA FE, NM 87504-2321 /USA
(505) 988-4418 / ORDERS ONLY (800) 243-5644 / FAX (505) 988-1025

Circus Americana
and
Other Poems

Michael Scofield

SUNSTONE PRESS

SANTA FE

FOR NOREEN

Contents

BURNED OUT

FRIENDS

I LOVE YOU

PREFACE

The following poem of mine pretty much says why at age seventy-eight I stay a writer:

> Inner worlds swirl when my outer
> world's a bowl, containing each
> morning like a prayer.
> The antics of all my subconscious
> fools—the love messes they tangle in—
> peel off the years, goose me
> from bed. The routine—
> breakfast, brushing,
> coffee—sees me
> to my desk by seven,
> blinds drawn. No sneak peak
> at *The New York Times*. No chitchat
> about the day's weather.

The arrangement of the eighty-one poems in this book creates a story arc. The first two sections—"Not Getting Along" and "Bewilderment"—explain the third section, "Burned Out." The last two sections, "Friends" and "I Love You" (love poems written to my wife), share reasons for soldiering on.

Between my second collection of poems, *Whirling Backward into the World*, and this one, I wrote three novels—*Acting Badly*, *Making Crazy*, and *Smut Busters*—a loose trilogy set in Santa Fe. The books came unbidden. My intent had been to concentrate on poetry. But President Bush's lies about why we needed to invade Iraq so upset me that my subconscious dictated the penning of stories dealing with what happens when a leader misleads.

When a head-of-household, a CEO, even a country's president misleads, those being led tend to obey the urgings of their own dark sides. That's the premise of the novels and many of the poems in the first part of this collection.

Santa Fe's Sunstone Press has been my publisher for ten years. Never in an adult lifetime of selling advertising for print, and writing and selling articles and books, have I worked with people like Sunstone's publisher, James Clois Smith, Jr., and his assistant, Carl Daniel Condit. Fellas, thank you for your savvy and for your strength. Thanks, too, to Sunstone's art director, Vicki Ahl, for intuiting how to maximize the come-on of covers and text. Special thanks to my friend, Russel Stolins, for guidance in formatting.

For you, dear reader, I wish only this: enlightenment (however false, however fleeting) and a few laughs.

—Michael Scofield
Santa Fe

ACKNOWLEDGMENTS

Many thanks to these journals for first publishing the following poems, sometimes in earlier versions:

Comstock Review: "Leopard," "What Love Is"

Eldorado Sun: "Hating May Cause Attention Deficit Disorder"

Diner: "Epiphany"

New Mexico Poetry Review: "Ways of Coping"

Red Rock Review: "Playtime"

Santa Clara Review: "Let's Change Reality, Okay?" "Nothing"

Serape: "Kabul on the Evening News"

Sin Fronteras: "B Minor Mass," "Concrete," "Our Love"

Weekly Alibi: "Jubilate"

EPIGRAPH

This tourists' blue-sky town is a
midden of tissue alps, squashed cans
of cola, spring-water empties,
latex gloves. Expect soon a din

of cottontails clinking
through Budweiser Lights and juncos
nesting in discarded bubblewrap unless
we name me Pied Piper of Trash.

Children, swallow your ibuprofen
for pollen, ready
your backpacks, we have a week
to give apricot blossoms

roads to pave. No more broken
glass for tulips to twist up
through, Big Slurp cups
to overturn, plastic bags to smother in.

NOT GETTING ALONG

ALL IN HER HEAD?

Made his eyes dangle
with a mess-kit spoon,
split open his skull
and ladled his brains,

yammers Lulijeta Krasniqi,
dizzy all day though she takes her pills.

Delirium, her granddaughter says,
Serbians marched the women away—

we heard only screams from
the one hundred four
village men plus
my husband and hers.

Outside, red ants blitz a broken-winged beetle.

To a Pulitzer-Prize Winner

You can write but oh, dear
God, the detail,
detail—what
eight spices you stir
into your curry,
what subtropical animal
your belt caused the death of.
The payoff's
not worth the wait—she lost
her baby, they divorced, end of story.

B MINOR MASS

Say AIDS, famine, smallpox, and war
slow our species' growth to zero—how many
lifetimes have we to enjoy
refilling birdbaths for the songs
of sparrows? Four lifetimes back

Bach spent a decade yanking straight
the curls of periwigs, wrenching
buttons from his velvet
waistcoats to glorify God and recreate
the mind, an orchard of vocalists thundering
into blossom—oh, silence coming, earth shining,
a blue and white pot.

SIAMESE TOWNHOUSES

Your heart's desire is puce and mine's
soft rose and the Homeowners Association
won't like either. *Tough titty.* Let's trade colors
halfway through, garages, bedrooms puce—
baths and kitchens rose—be twins. *Bug off.*
Single combat? *Spatulas or trowels?* We need
prison like a hole. *Let's buy the other out or burn
the fuckers down.* Good fences make good kindling.
Puce builds self-esteem.
Rose brings peace. *Choose your weapon.*

so don't hate the think-tanker
begging our Pentagon to pour
millions into microbes so genetically wrenched
they eat only the guts
of Palestinians. Weep
that this author of *Muscling-Up America's Will
to Build Peace*—when young—penned
couplets from a platform his mother pulleyed up
into their backyard eucalyptus.

Hear no smoker's hack, just "Mummy,
I've fallen on my tummy, come
quick."

LATE NIGHT TV

Says she loves him, says she
does not, no way. How
can this be? Love sequential?
Conditional? He pisses her off
when he snores, more
when he leaves the drainer
soggy with oat flakes.

She says the red mood
swoops down and hoods her,
binds her wrists, rends
her silent, has he noticed?

Says she hates him more than she
hates her father, who ripped to tatters
the Raggedy Andy her mother gave her
before scramming with the neighbor.
Can he match that, she wonders?

CIRCUS AMERICANA

We're going to invade and my tongue
tastes the rotten eggs of
gunpowder. Mow 'em down,
cut 'em to ribbons, corn hoe their women
and shish kebab their children. Can't you hear
our Cabinet's altar boys
storming the West Wing to watch
HDTV? Onward Christian
Medal-of-Honor winners while Sumerian masks
gawk in the Antiquities Museum
and washer-dryers rust in shops
awaiting their liberators.

Deepak would have us
hear our hearts beat
harmony, laughter,
love while I'm writhing,
reading of Afghans
training Dobermans to rape
soldiers who strung Afghans
by their noses?
Love if blindfolded and ears muffed,
that maybe I can do.

Hating May Cause Attention Deficit Disorder

My mind's packed with grenades—the stove's
stinking gas but where
did the phone go, where's the sponge
to sop up this honey
writhing with ants? Time passes so fast
I can't bathe in the eddies
of Bach's *Italian Concerto*. Add Ants-Gone
to the grocery list,
baggies for the mouse corpses furring the
fluorescent, add ripe peaches. Clamp
on the headset but where's the sponge, where's
my shotgun, where's that knife with the sawtooth blade?

DEAD END

Can clanging and foil
bunched like a ketchup-splotched fist

bounce toward the gutter from that Chevy enameled
in blue-and-yellow Jesus-and-Mary

roaring past our park like the purple limo

booked last week whose bullets dropped two marching
Mothers for Peace. Wind

disarms the fumes, and brake lights blush
at the round-the-corner screech—the wrap
that kept a burger hot

tumbling into a straggle of white-petaled
primroses, the Bud Light careening up our graveled road

toward the adobe marker reading *Private*

Speed Bumps 10 M.P.H. No Egress.

Santa Fe

Hearts do mend though snow
still gusts in May. It's the
cloudscapes that salve
past lives, lips-sealed children,
marriages we thought were salvageable
until the mailman came. The quiet
of these mountains—
like pillows, though the weather
spikes like mood.

Even evil Los Alamos can't turn
clouds' balm to acid rain
while meth-fomented drive-bys
peak. New Mexico's old-timers
plus Sufi, Tibetan, Muslim—
all of us hardwired to harm
but working hard to learn the
lessons of the clouds.

Kabul on the Evening News

Bombs? No. Twelve hundred pounds
of Pop-Tarts, wheat, and barley stew flatten
her corrugated-iron shack, mangy
hounds whooshing like missiles

out her windows, yelping past
the dangling spy, whose beard as furry
as their ears disappears
in telephone cable that yanks
him high, cratered eyes gaping

toward the cave where a smart-fused
bunker-buster turns granite
into Grape-Nuts, bouncing
through passageways until it shreds
the robed arch foe who uses his sleeve
to wipe his nose—pass me the popcorn, please.

CONCRETE

Despite my longing and
your tears, I still feel
no love, numbed

the night you stabbed
my setter's paw, myself
just back

from bedding a woman
other than your mother—
whom I wed to live

my parents' dream of perfect.
While you counsel battered
women, I kill mornings warming

cereal for the homeless. If you'll
recall us cuddling
under cottonwoods, I'll recall

you weeping in pink sleepers,
grabbing my cuff the evening
I walked out.

REORG

Let others dash
to war, you stay put
and lay down bricks,
though this is Tremor
Central—crevasses spread.
Stuff 'em full of frangipani,
train the footlong leaves
to slash through body bags,
hack and chop God's images, then
fill what's left with
eucalyptus, hear earth's
sighs, spring's clangor beating
swords to plowshares
while purple fragrance
allays the summer's burning.

BEWILDERMENT

CAN'T COUNT ON MUCH

That's Sichuan pepper reddening the calendar,
not shrimp (not pink)
spreading on the bamboo-shadowed gravel.

Yangjuan's cash crop (red peppers? shrimp?)
keeps kids in school. Though nothing
learnt can overturn
the bent to misperceive: her glance proves
she longs for sex? That man's unhappy

since he's scowling? That crow's a raven?
That raven's a crow? Pepper aids
digestion. Pepper clogs the bowels.

WHAT DREAMS MUST MEAN

is in us or beyond or nowhere.
Watch out for her, my publisher
says, *she'll fix dinner and her sausage casings
taste like rubber.* She?
Who? You or me
or both or neither? This morning's
starting like a dream: why's
that telephone jangling? Good tidings,
boring, bad, annoying? Who knows
if I don't answer? Who knows
if I do? Best not rely on
mirrors. Tea leaves neither. Don't
turn on the news.

of being human if what we say
is chatter? Like
Good to see you! (Not so good
when you start choking). Like
God is dead when my god, Fancy,
lives. Or seemed to
when I wrote this. But chatter
warms the cockles, fends off dread.
Like *I adore you.*

The apple drops
because earth charms it.
Gravity, what's that? (No one
knows though some expect to.)
Apple? Outer skin
and central core. Like a
baseball? No, you eat it.
Chatter, chatter, chatter.

ACTS OF RELIGIOUS COURAGE

That Islamic Albanian on the evening news
passed out watching a Serbian militiawoman
free his guts with a bayonet
because he wouldn't shout allegiance to
the Bishop of Pec.

And remember how Eleazer in "4 Maccabees"
refused to eat pork, though guards tore his shoulders
with ropes and piped nettles
in vinegar into his nose
until his ears oozed red?

Just how courageous does God need us to be?
I invested in Standard Oil and retired
a Catholic, though I do confess
that the daily effort to believe requires
Tums after taking the Eucharist.

Perhaps suffering for belief means
nothing—mostly He seems to want us
to populate. Last year a jackknifing flatbed
paralyzed our priest while his sister's belly
bulged with #7.

Uh Oh

Let's stand
on our heads to cheer
that frocked ladybug,
time our hurrahs to its twitching
batons—uh, oh, wren
has wriggled free, we forgot
his hood, what a mess
of song he makes
slamming the glass.

Do Not Bomb Children

I'm huddled sucking fumes
that sear my lungs,
Compassion for Iraqis
pressing my chest, nose
dribbling mucus
onto the muffler reddening
my throat as semitrailers,
rental vans, pickups sprouting
aluminum ladders,
spraying soot like flak
downshift off the signal
like the grinding
of bones. Judy jiggling
her *Honk If You Agree*
stalks drivers like an earmuffed
praying mantis.

Beeped replies
stutter from the intersection—
cacophony of an auto shop
but I don't want my car
fixed, don't want a car at all.

At a Recital of the Goldberg Variations

He hits the keys like a moneylender clacking
abacus beads—oh, Papa, scribbling notes
by candlelight, wouldn't your eyes pop
to hear this enthusiast, gardenias
in their cut-glass bowl
trembling near the keyboard?

HIS DAUGHTER AND SON BEG HIM BACK

but he won't return, not without
wailing, to the land of technological savvy

where lilacs scenting adobe walls

seem dreams. Though he picks his way
past syringes and beer cans, he blooms in Santa Fe,

his spirit's a well-tuned guitar.

Though his neck is wrinkling,
he sees sunrises blazing from fleabane—

he clicks castanets.

FOURTEENTH WAY OF LOOKING AT A BLACKBIRD

A man and a woman
are one.
A man and a woman and a blackbird
are one.
A lawyer puffing through metaphysics and the tick
burrowing through his black stocking
are one.
A white oak leaf and its fungus are one—like
the yellow eye among twenty
snowy mountains.

GRATITUDE PRAYER

Penning a tale no publisher
would touch, what's the point?
Porn, cocaine, homeless heroes who
smell bad—who'll read it?
Men read about ways
to get rich and women long
to cry. Why research

sleaze, crisscross half an acre of broken
glass, burnt elms, torn
sleeping bags, thistles, burrs? Why
buy a been-there, done-that informant
lunches? (Though I like the guy.
My tramps, too—their pluck.) But who

but a fool relishes eleven
rewrites? This longing
for perfection—useful?
Yet wallowing in
these characters' woes gives me
reason to rise before sunup every morning and
switch on the light.

Undressing in Front of a Fully Dressed Woman

is different in the dark. She

can appraise your goods no better
than you can gauge her reason for asking you
up. Do her fingers fumble her blouse
or grab a vase? Don't let her make your headache

worse by singing—why
is she clutching your face?
Salome? Or wants it all?
Find a light switch quick.

LAST RESORT

Marble flooring, guards, their boots and
ironed shirts and black-belt
cell phones, pedestals
bearing native bowls costing
twenty-five thousand, seventy-five thousand—
ten percent off if we stay. A lagoon-shaped
swimming pool's
slide (no children) near the four-star
eatery, its teepeed napkins linen, awaiting
master chef Tony's
maple-glazed salmon.

Down the stairs
to blare, slots complex as
video games, lights circling
twelve hundred screens,
human oddments spinning cherries,
sleeves to their elbows,
chins up to polish off
the last of their Miller Lites.

Of importance do we know any more
than the sheep on that Yangjuan
wall calendar trying to stay awake,
keep breathing? You can almost hear
the ticks feeding as they pick their ways
through wool—almost smell
the cigarette on the herder's lip. What's
it all about, Mgebbu? Food, propagating,
gratitude sometimes? Owning a straw
raincoat, ruminating the Mystery, those
blue cliffs we're all closing in on?

MEDITATION

Two centuries ago Papa Haydn
scribbled 53 piano sonatas, 205 trios,
25 masses, 23 operas, 104 symphonies,
21 concertos, 83 string quartets. Super
computer Cray X-MP can sum
800 million times a second. We know
what to do with Haydn's sonatas—
play them! But what to do about
X-MP's 39,751-digit prime? A 125-digit
prime is more than all subatomic
particles in the cosmos.

TIPS FOR ALLAYING GRIEF

Last night in group Julie pretended
that Mom still moves
around the house where Julie's planning
to sell Mom's quilts and silver
to end her grieving, sick
of squirting Murine
into smarting eyes. Sheila

confessed she's already practicing
her father's passing,
though he's still kicking his
heels up on Saturdays.
She's hoping not to suffer when he
breaks his back and begs her
to pull the tubes. Oh, gee,

I doubt whatever we do can stop us
from washing down razor blades
when the Ref calls time,
when sweetie, mom, pop, favorite
begonia, or Alaskan malamute roll over
and stay dead.

HALF HERE

You've gone
visiting
and I'm glad
to feel the cold
of loneliness
at my back.
That buzz—brain waves
or eternity
perking while I
pen nonsense or maybe
not, who knows?
Hundreds of tulips primping
for the revel
of your homecoming

MOST OF WHAT I'VE LEARNED

even kissing you
good morning and night
will die
with me, unlike
a flat-tail horned toad's
search for flies or
New Mexican primrose's flowering.

Violence, mostly, is what
passes down our genes,
the lust to love,
the *Look at me*'s. So what
that I keep my nails trimmed?

Once I'm gone who'll read
*Whirling Backward, Acting Badly, Smut
Busters, Making Crazy*? Why
should they? So little time for
art to compensate
for what we've had to open
our hearts to.

Two Hundred Years after Wordsworth's "Ode"

...gazing at a calendar's photo of yaks
surrounded by orchids on a slope
outside Yangjuan Village at
eleven thousand feet...

Did he who made the Lamb make
thee? Could be—or not—is the
question then and now when
colony collapse plagues not just
bees. Are we heading somewhere
back past birth in hopes that
after this the only way
is up? *There was a time when every
common sight to me did seem
apparelled in celestial light.* No, no,
they can't take that away, but do
until the mind becomes a grinding
engine spewing orchids, yaks,
*meadow, grove, and stream in glory
and the freshness of a dream.*

PASSING TIME

Out in the park I'm starting
to shiver but Bart, a grizzled
eighty, is dying
to show me scars on his neck and
in his armpit. Beaten
since birth by his mom
because Dad
beat her. They died, but *we live*—
Bart taps his temple.

Cold and weary
I wrap my ribs
listening to kids
on the jungle gym
shining in light
dying behind
three Siberian elms,
watch the moms
chattering while Bart
drones on.

EPIPHANY

To celebrate my sixty-fifth, we spoon the last
of cherries jubilee. The maitre d'
dims the lights, we rise to sway with the clarinet, my wife's hair

roars into flame. Shreds

of red from her white wave shimmy
toward the chandelier as drums
and bass exhilarate the reed. Wrenching free, she
pirouettes, the fire braids, her silk-clad arms

rise like a martyr's. She drops
to her knees, gives thanks
for the sign that she's esteemed, asks
her God to bless me. The maitre d' nods smiling,

runs for water.

HATE TO GO

Who to thank for sunlit morning glories?
Bad moods
bring up good ones.
It's springtime
for the Muslims
and the Bomb.
The planet's packed, time
to move on. But look!
That shrubby cinquefoil, spreading
golden wings.

COLOR COUNTS

Why are you drawing Schweitzer
and Jesus? *Posters for the peace march
later.* Yes, one must do something
to kill time—I'd hoped to see
The Strangler but violence cramps
my colon—may I help make posters?
*We need Marian Anderson and
Martin Luther King.* But they're black,
how about Buddha and Mother
Teresa? *No brown pencils.*

LEOPARD
—after Robert Stiver's photograph

Have I no choice than confront the harsh cough,
the green eyes—
endure the pain of sinews stretched
until night drops
to stop my screams?

God grant me
angels fluttering, children
swearing to change their lives—
Leopard dozing in the branches,
its belly content with dog.

Behind Closed Doors

Pablo Picasso,
Willem de Kooning,
what were you doing
to your women? Why did they
put up with it? Because they felt
the portraitures fit?

Dream On

The canales boast ice beards,
while indoors I'm frisky, describing
wind chimes ringing,
married this time
twenty-eight years.
In my ebb, all objects seem
awesome while organs pump,
absorb. Perhaps today
all will stay well if
I can keep rising off
my knees after prayer.

RONDANINI PIETÀ

Trapped in their marble mass as in
quicksand, Mary, chipped and
scarred, leans on Christ
sagging against her, forearm severed,
nose and penis smashed by the
aging sculptor when God bellowed,
*Earthly beauty turns
putrid, art is false solace, man's
pride.*

Jerking awake at midnight,
booted and smocked,
Michelangelo snatches
his hammer, coughing stone dust
swarming like gnats, and hacks away
at his passion for flesh in a last try
to please God.

Escaping the Now

How I long to sing
like Césare Siepi,
brandishing my sword,
instead of sweating
after nightmares spawn
whirligig eyes. Dear Césare,
does the Don ever wonder
if he'll wake, grip gone—
too much slaughter,
hearts brought to their knees,
passion changed to venom,
sweetened by greed?

What's it like turning ontology
into staccato partitas while straining
on the pot and what's it like
hearing your lover gasp
when your tower leans and she climbs on top
to straighten its logic out?

EMOTIONAL HUNCHBACK,

lugging books to sell,
big toe birthing a corn,
I remember other scenes:

Sister's tantrums, Mom's incontinence
of kisses, Auntie's parades
in bra and panties, Uncle's Parkinson's.
They told me be a good boy, be a
big boy, write stories for children.

SECOND CHILDHOOD

Loved my grandpa, treated me
his equal, so loved to peddle
perfumes he made, his green bean
splitters (bamboo and razor blades)
door-to-door, yes, ma'am, my grandpa
made these. Love my publisher and his
assistant, they say my poems
worth showing off, so love to sell
their greeting cards around the Plaza,
shop to shop. Yes, sir, yes, ma'am,
a dollar each, delivery no charge.

Mistrusted Mother and Dad, their
push-pull caring, so penned
by flashlight *The Bloody-Eyed Bats
of Mars*. Mistrust Uncle Sam, his
gaudy hat, those smiling lies, so penned
the novel, *Acting Badly*, then penned
Making Crazy. Wonder if after the next election
I'll be writing a sequel to
The Bloody-Eyed Bats or looking
for more perfumes to peddle,
books, and cards.

BURNED OUT

Capitalistic Fix

That Amanda's ditched me for some
technogeek perfecting a Riesling-based
vodka to save his biophys bigwigs whose Napa
vineyard sales have tanked

is why you see me
lolling in these
ylang-ylang scented bubbles, careful not
to soak my daily
just-say-no-to-drugs
Wall Street Journal high
folded at the tub's far end. Soon

I'm gonna hatch my own
golden egg like Charles Flinn his
transgenic blue-and-white
guppies flashing
fluorescent tickers or Manny Mooser's swine
that shit
phosphate pearls—I'm thinking here

Iraq: show those sand niggers how a
decoded Koran dictates
turning corpses into boob enhancers
and nylon headgear for the guys.

WOE

This poem should be a painting,
a video! Detailing extreme
distress at the bookstore's podium,
facing all those empty
chairs, us three nifty
in orange sweatshirts,
the publisher claiming
I Don't Mind, his assistant tidying
the display, and me, the rep, seeking
one warm body
to buttonhole. But there's only Myndie
ready to pass out
plastic-cupped frappés,
plus one gaunt poet who hopes to read,
and one who's brought his folks.

UNCLE!

A newspaper ad claims a doctor can sever
my head for $50,000 and freeze it
until science can pump my
DNA into a robust corpse—ageless forever,
given water and food, but look
how fast we're doing earth
in. Perhaps for another
$50,000 I can beam up to Mars.

Apricot blossoms
in the Unitarian churchyard,
Beethoven's *Grosse Fuge* when I'm feeling
transcendent: easy. But give me
a no-lick stamp that won't stick,
our cat puking grass balls
onto the bedspread, and I come
undone. Endlessness? Not a prayer.

BURNED OUT,

overdone—bail out,
washed up, high time to abandon
scribbling,
man overboard, good
riddance, try another tack:
mail sorter, feather dusterer, closet organizer,
tulip maintenance.

SEESAW

Hallelujah, gonna die, done and
done in,
ash, that's it,
no more metaphors, fine
clothes parading
being, no more
meaning—out
like a light but oh,
forsythia flickering, Scotch broom
spreading its honey, my love's
body, lips open, thighs
wide and oh, the
feast of Thomas Mann's
Doctor Faustus, sweet
incomprehensibility,
the horror of no more anything,
the angst I might be wrong—
the relief.

WAYS OF COPING

Guzzling brandy from the bottle,
our professor dunks us
full immersion into his faith
that we must fashion
works of art to soothe a disillusioned
Deity.
      My art's a souped-up ruby roadster
that mornings hurtles
into head winds, changing me to Loki,
Lord of Laughter.

DEATH BY SELF-DISCIPLINE AVERTED

Such a thrill to sit & write
nonsense while the espresso machine
screams. Bye-bye
rising at five, whisking the mind
to la-la lands
peopled by malcontents doing
dirt. Now's the chance
to let the pen drift toward verbs chasing
nouns, who cares?
Few care about the stories
I've slaved over—who wants to read
about fat mortgage brokers
or high-tech alcoholics or homeless
composers or gay bodybuilders?
Not me. Plunk
this scribbler, pencil, pad, & Americano,
into a chair under the fan
at Downtown Subscription and let him
slide into evening
patterning pages with chicken tracks.

EXHAUSTED

by dreams of blooming
waterless, trying
to get there by running
in place. The gauge
reads empty, bark beetles
gnaw the piñons brown. Mother,
cradle me, I'm tired of nursing you.
Daddy! Where have you gone?
The air got warm, the clouds
are curdling, words no longer
mean. Why does that peony
anger me? Lobotomy—I crave
the joy.

LET'S CHANGE REALITY, OKAY?

Moon, don't wane
like my uncle did of Parkinson's,
shrinking to a slavering
smile. Don't wax
like my sister's mind, a piñata strewing
coins for psychoanalysts. Enough
of cycles—all is gone to all
is well, is gone, is well, is gone.
You stay full.

What Haircut?

Snick, snick, Robert
the barber trims
gray shocks to fighting length.
I've got to sell more *Acting Badly*'s,
battle America's
depression, mine that
last month's haircut seems so
long ago, seen
through a scrim. Have I grown
so old? Half
the Plaza's shops have closed,
landlords plunge rents
forty percent. Time for me
to pretend
everything's easing—
sell books, sell cards, praise
buds on the cottonwoods,
serve lunches at the shelter.

THEME AND VARIATIONS FOR TOY PIANO

I shall play the tune
as it is written—
do re la la mi so ti fa

But shouldn't I play it so we
can fall in love?
la la mi fa do so ti la

You'd rather throw stones?
so re mi do la la ti fa

Then guess who longs for death—
so fa ti re la la do la la mi—

as you attend orioles heralding the sun—
re mi so la la fa ti do

Loree O'Leighlee enjoins me
to pray, says knees
are for scraping, oh, whisk me away

I Don't Know How Others Write

For me it's slog, revise, blaspheme,
tear into confetti, sleep
fitfully, double dose on fiber,
watch children playing in the park,
ask my wife to read it, rewrite,
delete, ask my wife to read it
and when she claims a migraine,
ask the gerbil.

LAST RITES

Fat is how my father went—
Mother, hunched. Fat and hunched
don't merit A's although
I'd love to say *How swell
to see you both.* Love—
I think—is what I feel, loss
that they've gone down and I'm still
treading, though my mind seems
young and memory objects
to what the mirror shows.

Their middle age I can't recall
except her pleas to come
to church, and Father's rage
to find no net to keep me caught
in the family business,
so maybe I'm much better off
a lonely man today.

I HAVE A FEW QUESTIONS

but none in the morning when
the woman in linen
brings scones
for us both. Yes to a banana, too,
and trial kiss to learn
how best
to seal our lips when the sun
winks out.

FRIENDS

SHOCK WAVE

Neon stockings to the knees? Please
don't tease. Oh, geez, shock of hair
out to there? Culture shock, snow
on the go—dress your age, Madge,
dump the bourbon, cadge a cup of
Postum, chug-a-lug. Chockablock
with death and you've decided
shock jock? Aftershock for me, babe,
blab happiness all you like.

My Friend James

Why can't I write love-of-nature poems
like him, bouquets of them?

Bud Light and Crystal Geyser empties
lurk where I look, lottery tickets, condoms.

Nebraska's a mere state away—its grass
adds shag to how many Minutemen
snugged in silos, gyros whirring?

Dr. Zhou's acupuncture bucks James up.
Zhou just cost me cash.

James feels sure he'll reappear a village bard
in Yemen.

PLAYTIME

Earthly paradise means
Imagination—that cholla blooms in January,
that Tibetan girl with polio
frolics in Monsignor Patrick Smith Park.
How we cluck at Downtown
Subscription, ho ho ha, dreaming up
schemes to make successors
to the Hula Hoop, Pet Rock. Oh, my dears,
were it true: more laughter, fewer meds;
more hugs, less of flesh's itch.
Smash the mirror that shows the neck
wrinkling. But what to do about
the pain of rising from a chair?
Nothing rash for now. We have pens
to play in, tea to sip, each other to envision
communing where Anasazi lived high
in caves—before drought forced them
to quit their coops and fly.

Homage to Dana Levin: a Cento

And every Friday there would be a cricket trilling endlessly
      against the din of traffic—
it legged the air ceaselessly where no one could hear it.
I would stand right next to it and watch the traffic stream.

You want to get in and then get out of the box—
      sunray cutting the dark cloud in two, that lucky lit patch
      of land.
When the door between the worlds opened
      you ceased to be a ghost.

The world asked for change, so you looked for the man
      shaped like an anchor,
he was standing with his dog, his great big German shepherd, he kept it
      tight on its leash.
      Blood-red beacon in the dark.
      The milky pearl.
At the top of the milkweed, pod
      about to unfold.

In the early morning you walked out—
      and the light said, Be mine.

The cento above consists of lines from Dana Levin's *In the Surgical Theater* and *Wedding Day*.

THE ARTIST

Four hundred years next door to her—
phony deeds of sale, enslaving
Native Americans, gunning down
Anglos, dealing smack for kickbacks—
form backdrops

to her watercolors, the blues
and oranges of Abiquiu, lovegrass
in snow, the hope they show:
pig wallows turned into ponds
for skating, fence posts partying,
rickety homes and rickety barns
reborn. Out of the house she

romps with Maddie, beloved
mutt perfuming the neighbor's
family tree, then in again to
swirling suns and apricots,
giant pears and thunderstorms,
pastels flowing into icy streams.

ALTERNATE ETHICS

He's my friend and you want to beat
him with that stick because he's
my friend and you're not?
You'll never catch him,
he's about to pass
the buoy. Hurl your stick, go on,
I'll bellow and he'll dive. So many people
brandishing sticks...sure,
threaten me, I'm available. Though I'll say nothing
you want to hear, do nothing
but crumple. Want to see how I've lettered
my chest? *Too many people,*
resistance is evil.

IT APPEARS, YEP, WE'RE ALL STILL HOPPING

Why did the older poet
keep extracting
earwax? Why gallop
through *William Bonney* slurring
her words? I preferred

the younger's requiem
for New Orleans,
*Bumping Along the Back Roads to
Love.* But drove home
shook: the gallery's downlights

showcased Lena, humped-over
poet back to life,
like Anna with her graying
updo, Lucian and his checked bandanna,
Lauri's wrinkled skirt—fading

memories who had this evening
sprung from their sarcophagi: *Hi, Michael,
ho, Michael, third book before
Christmas, Lauri's third by spring.*
We five last hugged

four years ago, disbanding like hippies
slipping off braided rings—
Lena lapsing into bitterness,

Anna wordless
at retreats, Lucien in Reno expending
his son's sanity, Lauri down to Albuquerque,
Santa Fe too boutique.

JEREMIAH DANCING

Eighteen-hundred quotations from literature,
twelve-hundred bites from classical music,
thousands of paintings, sculptures, buildings—

Charles G. Bell's forty-video, three-millennium
passion.

"Against the cancerous waste of this planet
uproot the future! Set
entropy upon itself
while protons and electrons twist
into a Sufi dance."
As Beatrice beckons in *The Commedia*,
as three-faced Buddha chuckles at gout,
as *Otello* collapses to violins,

so Bell shouts, "We can't
accept the running down, we must
recreate a humanism,
such a blaze as turns the wheel,
radiant as Lear
when he sees the love-truth that
Cordelia lives."

I LOVE YOU

IN YOUR ARMS FOREVER
—after Dominique Boisjoli's painting

Beside our hut of rushes yanked
from the banks of this muck-
shored lake, we'll nurture rhododendrons—
watch crimsons wafting toward
that blue glacier, its boulders
pillows until the crush preserves us from
the bitterness of age.

AGING TOGETHER

Twenty-four years—adults now,
no? Though kissing
makes me think of
high school: can't swallow,
arrhythmia, commotion
in the boiler. Your flesh,
wrinkling, gives such solace
I pretend we're Siamese
even when you run downstairs
because I'm snoring. Folie
à deux? What else to call
the idiocy of planning for who
goes first? Eat, don't drink,
be merry, stay in touch,
be grateful...you got it, kid.

NETFLIX NOURISHMENT

Vigilant all day, not to sneak peeks
at the paper nor the twelve o'clock

news nor
boot up the *Times* nor log

onto *Slate.* Nor in the car to
turn on talk shows rather than

classical music. At dinner
not discuss our parents' apparent

mistakes, our own,
our childrens'. But then, soft in robes

and snuggies, to cuddle
on the sofa and slip in a disk

from Netflix. Film noir's
Richard Widmark slugging the turncoat,

Richard Conte embracing Gene Tierney
watching the evil hypnotist

bleed. Black-and-white bad guys
battling good guys. Stark human beings!

Suspense! Drawn-out scenes! Reel love
saved from the lost-and-found

after sixty years, all scripted, the blood
dabbed, the false tears gently

nudged into ducts
naturally full to bursting.

NOTHING

I could do about Carmelita Lopez
knifing her boyfriend through the neck in the nave

as he tried to yank
cocaine from her jacket and nothing

I could do about our Pentagon rushing
200,000 bayonets into Kuwait hoping

to transform Saddam into a sieve except
summon the long-ago notes of cuckoos

above Villa Pitiana, the brook's
gurgle under the cobblestones,

bees whirring in red poppies, my wife
on tiptoe whispering how

she longed to make love.

TIME PASSING

Sweep to keep
the tiles clean, bathe
to stop the skin from flaking,
deeply dream of bones to hold
our bodies steady so we can scan
the peaks for snow—
it's spring again? Let's believe ourselves
Moon Mountain while seasons
come and go.

WHY JOY,

deep like carrots
corkscrewing through
caliche, roots of
pricklepoppy, ragwort, fleabane
while our colons
cramp, argon lasers
zap our eyes—why joy?
Because you sigh
when I touch your cheek.

FOR NOREEN

Sixty-nine years? No!
You appear in orange shoes,
striped jerseys. We make candlelight
love. Two decades of cuddling
can't have passed! Pain binds us like gifts
exchanged. How our hearts
twist when our children fall. I need
always the longing for laughter
in your green eyes, the deep
rejoicing so far.

Happy Hour

What a beautiful time
to write, robins fluttering
in their bath, an Anna's hummer probing
the catmint, no gusts, no barks,
a flock of O'Keeffe puffs coasting.

How about describing

our twenty-first anniversary
dinner in the hotel garden,
its teepee, fountain, the loudmouthed
realtor limping off,
freeing us for whispers and linen napkins,

tenderized elk, California
tangerines. High walls
muffling city sirens. An Indian flute
flitting like the hummer. No glass
to reflect our flesh.

FOR OUR 20TH ANNIVERSARY

We've toughened so and yet
when you kiss my eyelids
I go mushy, wish
we had the wherewithal to hop back
into bed, lead lives that servants could
provide, though somehow
struggling with no-strings love
tempers us to deal with hospitals
and maybe (no way!)
death. I love you as the juniper
the piñon, lungs the heart,
and whatever time past twenty years
we have to say good night and then
good morning is
second-by-second blessed.

WHAT LOVE IS

Love is bright
feathers, wind stroking ricegrass,
breath on your hair. Love is
freckles, pinwheel sunflowers,
that green hummingbird.

Love is where
you are, love is my sadness
that freckles darken, wind snaps
grasses, flowers gray.

But love is also pairs of ravens
soaring under storm clouds
round the year.

JUBILATE

Kissing you is like
plunging into
blue-blossomed sage,
a hummingbird whirr
every new penstamon
cloud-blooming day.

LOVERS STREAKING PAST SEVENTY

A race to see who'll die
first, not be the loser
left to cope, though strangely
we're both struggling
to tramp the stepper,
endure the back roll,
while popping Lexapro

to master migraines, Klonopin,
Lorazepam to tag-team
toss and turns. Why not yearn

to go? What if
death's more
painful? We love
to cuddle, watch Netflix disks,
wait for birthday free
desserts at Pranzo,
kiss the nights away.

Though sometimes I think
I should have been
a pair of ragged claws scuttling across the floors
of silent seas.

OUR LOVE

is like watering autumn ashes and Russian olives
in this drought's lack of snow,

agreeing over soup and toast to pull
our knit caps down,
tramp into the chill to rake

holes in cedar mulch, watch water
gush from hoses, wind straightening
blue grama's curls while the battery-powered radio
propped against the rock wall you built
heats the air with Beethoven's Ninth—

wrens in the junipers twitching their tails.

UNCONDITIONAL LOVE

Moments pop like tortoises
from nests in Galápagos
sand, scrambling
to keep the stump-
winged cormorants
from gobbling them up
before reaching
the mothering waves.

May they multiply—like
flashes in your hair, your
touches—and may I see
these moments as garnets
in stone, love poems
springing from woe.

www.ingramcontent.com/pod-product-compliance
Lightning Source LLC
Chambersburg PA
CBHW031354060726
47590CB00007B/2777